Children's Education
in Community

Children's Education in Community

The Basis of Bruderhof Education

Selections from the Writings of
Eberhard Arnold

PLOUGH PUBLISHING HOUSE

Published by Plough Publishing House
Walden, New York
Robertsbridge, England
Elsmore, Australia
www.plough.com

FIRST EDITION: 978-087486-164-8
SECOND EDITION: 978-087486-836-4

Edited and translated from the German by
Winifred Hildel and Miriam Mathis

A catalog record for this book is available from the British Library.
Library of Congress Cataloging-in-Publication Data

Arnold, Eberhard, 1883–1935.
  Children's education in community: the basis of Bruderhof education.
  1. Christian education of children. 2. Children—Religious life. 3. Bruderhof
Communities. I. Title.
BV1475.2.A75   370.11′4   76-27728

Whoever seeks me shall find me in children,
for there will I be made manifest.

Lord's Saying in Hippolytus

Contents

Foreword   ix

Foreword

THIS SELECTION of passages from articles, meetings, and letters by Eberhard Arnold (1883–1935) was made after his death, at a time when there were many newcomers in the Bruderhof and the second generation was already taking an active part in the life of the brotherhood. Parents and teachers wanted a resource to help them return to the foundation on which our education is built.

From the very beginning in 1920, when Eberhard and Emmy Arnold first started to live in community with Emmy's sister Else von Hollander and others, they took in needy children and brought them up with their own five children, then two to ten years old. Eberhard Arnold had been called by Jesus to a life of Christian discipleship at the age of sixteen and remained faithful to his early call until his death. With his wife, Emmy, he lived a life of service to Christ, first in the evangelical movement of that time, from 1907 until 1915, then in the German Student

Christian Movement, as its secretary, and later as director of its publishing house.

The community life he then helped to establish in Sannerz in 1920 was an answer to the outcry and longing of young people in particular, who were disillusioned and desperate in the aftermath of World War I. The shaking events of that war, the collapse of Russia and the Russian revolution, the catastrophe in Germany, and the terrible need there and in other countries made many Christians seriously examine their own lives and ask, "Do Christians of our time really follow the commandments of Jesus? Do we live in keeping with the Sermon on the Mount and the events of Pentecost, as we read in Acts 2:44 and Acts 4:2?"

These questions found various answers, one of them being the new beginning in Sannerz, which for the first two years was the center of quite a widespread movement. The sad consequences of the war were still keenly felt, so from the very beginning the little group felt a strong urge to open their hearts and homes to orphaned children or children from broken families. When the wider movement subsided, there were more rooms available at Sannerz and more children were accepted.

Eberhard Arnold expressed his ideas about true Christian education of children in several printed articles.

But there also are many important passages in transcripts of meetings and in Eberhard's correspondence, because the education of children was and is a central part of a brotherly and sisterly life. The present selection includes only a few of these, together with extracts from his published works.

To this day, in all its schools and children's departments, the Bruderhof continues to hold firmly to the direction outlined here. All Bruderhof communities welcome guests and coworkers who wish to come and share our life with us for a time. Contact information for each community can be found at bruderhof.com.

The Editors

I

What Is a Child's True Nature?

Only in the context of the whole life of our church community can we recognize the basis of our education and reach an understanding for the nature of the child we wish to educate.[1]

WHEN CHILDLIKE HEARTS are moved, it is the Holy Spirit who moves them. The child's life represents a new beginning in the light. To be a child means to make a new beginning.

THE GOSPEL OF JOHN loves the light of eternal life. It says, "Believe in the Light, that you may be made children of the Light." This is the most wonderful thing anyone could say about children. Children love the light; they do not like darkness. They hunger for life and thirst for light. They have no joy in the things of darkness. A true child loves the light and wants to get to it. He loves everything

---

1 Headings and passages in italics are by the editors.

that light reveals in nature. But he loves even more deeply the divine light of God.

EVERYTHING BELONGS to God; therefore everything belongs to the children. They are God's children, truly children of God, the children of God's spirit, who creates all things.

WE WANT TO BRING the little children very close to Jesus. In their nature lies just that which belongs to the kingdom of God.

OUR WORK WITH CHILDREN rests on the faith that the living Christ wishes to arouse from within each person all that is good in the way of decisions and abilities. The less the powers of hatred hold sway over a man, the more open his heart is to the spirit of peace and unity. So we concern ourselves in a special way with children, because they are not yet bound to the powers of evil to such an extent as adults; for good powers lie latent in the child, waiting to be awakened. All brothers and sisters are ready to help the children, but in particular those who share the life of the children inside and outside the school.

A Child Is Trusting

A CHILD trustingly accepts everything we give him, not to take possession of it but to become absorbed in it. The child does not feel any barriers between himself and the great world around him. In the very act of receiving, he gives himself. A small child does not separate himself from what he experiences. He senses what is given to him as part of the great world in which he becomes absorbed.

A Child Believes in Forgiveness

THIS IS THE CHILDLIKE SPIRIT: every child feels with perfect security that his father and mother will forgive him endlessly, no matter how many times he does something wrong. It would never occur to a child that the forgiving love of his father and mother might come to an end because he was naughty too many times.

A Child Is Outspoken

GENUINE CHILDREN will tell us immediately what they feel. As long as we let them be children, they will say what they do not like. They will not keep something quiet to a person's face and then talk about it behind his back. Cowardly deception is unchildlike. Real children are completely open; they are always ready to reveal whatever is in their hearts.

A Child Is a Free Person

CHILDREN ARE FREE, truly free. All children are free!
They must never become the property of father or mother,
much less of anyone else. Any action that deprives a child
of his freedom is a despising and degrading of the child.

God's heart loves little children and his eye is upon
them. He sees in them his own childlike spirit. Therefore
we must honor God in children; we must honor his
messengers in them.

A Child Has an Innate Religious Feeling

IN CHILDREN WE FIND a capacity for trust, justice,
and self-forgetful enthusiasm that we ourselves have lost.
This quality is what Jesus means when he says, "You must
become like little children."

Children experience the mystery of what is sacred
and divine, though of course in quite a different way
from adults. The child has no knowledge of religious
dogma or of the established form of church services.
But he experiences the mystery of sacred things because
he is free from thoughts about his little self – free from
self-observation – free to take into his heart the mystery
of all life. He senses the light of God behind the stars
that are kindled in the sky; in the wind he senses the

soaring of angels. He senses the living creative Spirit when he sees the flowers swaying in the breeze. He senses the beauty and strength of God's spirit in the splendors of nature. In people's love for one another and in the love of his own heart, he senses the mystery of God's love, the source of life.

FOR A REAL CHILD, love is creative joy in whatever he loves. In this love he abandons himself to the things that bring him joy. That is why the child can show a trust hardly ever found in us adults. The child is a trusting being, made for community.

A Child Has a Sense of Social Justice

EVERY REAL CHILD is a social being with an instinctive sense of justice, which urges him to help anyone who is worse off than he is. In a living organism, in a body united within itself, no cell lives for itself. Each one freely serves the others. So-called natural selfishness, even in children, is a disease or period of temptation and must be overcome. It contradicts the child's enthusiasm, which shows itself in his unselfish devotion to others and his natural feeling for justice.

ANY EDUCATING must be guided by the basic qualities inherent in every child: faith and trust, wonder and reverence, and self-forgetful surrender. These qualities of the true child actually reveal to us what man's true nature should be.

A Child Is an Individual

Modern educators maintain that every child must be given individual guidance and personal understanding. Therefore parents, teachers, and educators must lead each child with an understanding for his individual needs.

WE RESPECT the personality and uniqueness of each child in the light of something deeper than the purely personal, for this leads through the development of the individual to community, which is beyond the personal. In this way, individual abilities become serviceable for the whole. The specific gifts of every single child should be recognized and helped to develop along the lines of his true vocation. In the deeper sense, this must and will lead to loving service of the community of humankind, to the uniting of all the special characteristics of each one. Our community education therefore means doing justice to each child in the unfolding of all the abilities given to him. Under no circumstances should we force on him anything that is not given him at birth, that does not come from his own heart as his spiritual life awakens, that is not newly begotten and born in him through God. Guiding children toward a vocation has to be different for every single child; it will then be decisive for his whole life and will prepare him for his calling in practical service.

WE CANNOT MOLD our children to conform to our own wishes. The only true service to our children is to help them become what they already are in God's thoughts. Each child is a thought in the mind of God, and we should not try to mold a child according to our own ideas for his development. That would not be true service to the child. We will be able to do that service only if in each child we grasp the thought God has had for this very child from all eternity, and still has and will always hold to. This thought of God is the holy "Thou Shalt" for this child. God knows what this child is meant to be. This is the service of the church, of the parents, of all of us: to allow the child to become what this particular child is meant to be according to God's original thought. And here again, we need the religious intuition that enables us to grasp this thought of God, as yet apparently hidden from us – to grasp it more and more clearly from day to day, from moment to moment, from year to year. Then the molding of the child is not something we undertake. Rather, our service consists precisely in helping with the molding God has in mind. That is the secret of service.

A Child's Heredity

Every child is unique, but every child is born into a family whose characteristics – positive and negative – are handed down to him. How should we see this question of heredity?

THERE CAN BE no doubt that even the smallest child bears within him something from his parents that burdens him. And yet a small child is in quite a different situation from us adults with regard to his inherited inclination toward evil. The basic difference is that the child has not yet made a conscious decision for evil. His inheritance from parents and forebears of godlessness, antisocial forces, bad traits, and bad experiences is a burden on him. But this inheritance has not yet matured into deed. That is the fundamental difference between children and adults. Therefore we are right in speaking of the innocence or guilelessness of children, which is almost the same as sinlessness. If we really love children and live with them, we will see in any child the world we have left behind.

IT WOULD NEVER occur to us to think of children as being perfectly good. On the contrary, we know that they too are assailed by the forces of selfishness and untruthfulness.

THERE IS NO QUESTION that children, though not yet burdened by the bitter experiences of adulthood, do carry a need within them. It is here that faith in Christ sets in, in which all children are under grace. Because Christ has reconciled the whole world, he has taken away from all children the inherited misery of godless isolation.

When Does Childhood End?

AS SOON AS THE CHILD has consciously and willfully done evil, he has ceased to be a child.

THERE IS NO RULE for the age when this catastrophe occurs. The end of childhood, like the nature of the child, remains a mystery.

SO THERE IS no set time for the conscious struggle of the spirit against evil to begin. But in a certain critical year in the life of every child, this struggle leads to a devastating collapse of the former picture of childhood.

When this happens, all those who are responsible for the child's upbringing need alert hearts, active love, and real sharing in the child's experience. Along with the child, they are gripped by the danger that menaces him, not in the sense of knocking the child into shape from outside, but of taking up a fighting position within the child and with the child. Then this crisis will serve to strengthen the child so that he can himself take up the fight against evil and conquer it. This strength is the Spirit of the same Christ who has discovered and redeemed the nature of the child.

2

What Is Education?

Education Is Guidance

WE SPEAK OF EDUCATION in the sense of guidance, because we believe that children, lacking experience of life and therefore of evil, need the guidance that recognizes immediately the dangers threatening their souls, and then challenges them to fight against evil. Evil can be seen in a will that is covetous, that has turned away from God, and that acts according to human self-will.

OUR EDUCATION builds on trust in what is good and genuine, which grows alongside other extremely dangerous forces in the child and develops a strong, determining influence. Seen deeply, it is trust in the voice of God, which rises up in every child as a desire for community and as joy in purity, truth, and love. In daily life this trust is shown as reverence for this one thing that counts in all children. For us, educational community means the mutual stimulation of the best at work in each soul, especially in the undeveloped soul. Education means awakening the child to what alone is important, which comes to life in the depths of the heart.

AND YET it would be seriously wrong to conclude that there is no struggle in a child's life, no temptation to evil. The insight that Jesus gives us into the nature of the child shows us how alarming it is when the will to evil appears in a child and drives him to action. The important thing is to guide children so that their ability to give themselves freely is awakened and strengthened. It is important to occupy them with what is good, to interest them in the things of God, and to fill them with the strength that comes from these things. The free will must not be left unprotected to fall prey to evil. It must be won over for the good. Everything depends on whether we start this work of love, this work of awakening, at the point where the child is still really a child.

Education is not a matter of arguing with the child or crushing him with criticism, nor is it heartless condemnation or commands given without trust that they will be obeyed. Working with children means trusting, stimulating, and lending a helping hand. It means seeing the real and genuine childlike nature in each child. It means appealing to this childlikeness again and again and continually strengthening it. Love for the child supports and affirms his childlike nature. Through this love, new forces of good constantly strengthen the reality of this childlikeness, so that the child does not fall into conscious evil acts.

HERE WE SEE the purpose of our education: to lead children to unity, that is, to God's idea and God's will for men on this earth.

What Is Expected of the Educator?

ANYONE WHO WANTS to live with children must first of all recognize his own incapacity for justice in the deepest sense.

HOW DIFFICULT educating children is for us human beings, who are not free of sin, and what a responsibility! Only wise men and saints are fit to be educators. Our lips are unclean. Our dedication is not without reservation. Our truthfulness is broken. Our love is not perfect. Our kindness is not disinterested. We are not free of loveless-ness, possessiveness, and selfishness. We are unjust.

So it is the child who leads us to the gospel. If we look at our task with the children, it is quite clear that in view of the holiness of the task we are too sinful to bring up even one single child. This recognition leads us to grace. Without the atmosphere of grace, no one can work with children. Only one who stands like a child before God can educate children, can live with children.

"You must become like children." Like children, you must live in the presence of grace. You must learn wonder. In the knowledge of your own smallness, marvel at the greatness of the divine mystery that lies hidden in all things and behind all things. Only then can we be given the vision of this mystery, a vision that makes us forget ourselves because it overwhelms us with the greatness of the cause. Only those who look with the eyes of children can lose themselves in the object of their wonder.

EDUCATING MEANS struggling shoulder to shoulder with the children under one leader, Jesus Christ. Not that the educator fights the child or the pupil fights the teacher in their common struggle against lovelessness and untruthfulness. That is impossible. The real struggle can begin only when we have realized that we all sit on the same bench and are all in need of strength from above.

There can be no fight against the evil emerging in a child unless we first sit on the same bench with him, unless we first win one another's love and trust. Then and only then can we tackle the common enemy from a united front.

IT TAKES GREAT SENSITIVITY and a truly childlike spirit to guide children in the deepest and innermost things. This must not be done by anyone who has not already recognized the will of the Spirit for the child. True children have a deep reserve about holy things.

AS EDUCATORS we need daily guidance by the Spirit of Light. It is he who uncovers, combats, and casts out everything in ourselves and the children that brings darkness, before it gains dominion over young, sensitive hearts.

MAY HE WHO CONQUERED DEATH be our children's champion and leader! He himself is our strength. The educator's task is to point to him in word and action, in will and way.

What Is the Task of Education in a Christian Community?

A LIVING EDUCATION belongs in the midst of a living church community. Therefore the children's community is part of the adults' community of faith, where people live in the spirit of true brotherhood and service.

In a church community, where all-embracing love goes into action in the fight against self-will and possessiveness, all childlike qualities can flourish and grow to maturity, developing the powers to work and serve humankind. Here, the children's life is determined by their holy inner need for faith. Therefore it is guided by the power of faith living in the church. Here the parents, the educators, and the children themselves are truly functions of the living, all-inclusive unity of the church. The church's spirit of faith and love is the whole that transcends the individual. Its binding, uniting power permits the child to really be a child and, in the holy fight, saves him from fatal isolation. This power is more than the shared economy of the family; it is more than the limited common interests of blood ties. Here the child is drawn into those important activities, interests, and concerns that will make up the fabric of his life when he enters the adult world.

WHILE THE SPIRITUAL, emotional, and physical character of father and mother have a tremendous influence on unborn and newly born children, the educators and the whole community have just as great an influence. The strongest element in education is example. Children are led almost irresistibly by the examples they see and experience. They should experience examples filled with spirit and life. Therefore it is true that not only our teachers and educators help to mold the children's lives but also the community as a whole.

THE SERVICE OF TEACHER sums up the whole task of the church toward the children: the service of the word and the service of steward, for the children.[2] This service is one of the highest things in the church.

IF WE UNDERSTAND a little of what has been said here, we will have to realize that in any community whose members serve one another in love as brothers and sisters, the children must come first, the more so, the more they are true children.

2 A "servant of the word" (pastor) has a special responsibility for the inner life of the church and for bringing to expression the living Word of God given to the church. The steward is the community's financial manager.

The Working Together of Teachers and Community Is Essential

IT IS EXTREMELY IMPORTANT that there should be an active contact and understanding between the children's community and the community as a whole, especially the brotherhood (all committed members, men and women). From time to time the children – especially the older ones – should eat with the adults; these mealtimes will be devoted completely to the children. We must see to it that through the school principal the brotherhood keeps in touch with the children's community, in the work and in other ways. We should not try to do this in a forced and arbitrary way, but together with the responsible teachers we should find ways that will allow the brotherhood and the rest of the community to maintain a deep and lively contact with the children's community.

THE TEACHERS must work together as a team and meet frequently, at least once a week. Unless there is a regular sharing among the teachers they will have no discernment of the children's inner situation, no oversight of their progress in school, and no insight into the children's community as a whole. For the joy of the whole community, the school teachers should arrange often that the children sing to us, recite poetry, or report about a special experience; they should display the children's artwork or share other expressions of the school, preschool, or kindergarten activities. I do not think anyone will be bored. In this way everybody's interest in the children's community will be kept joyful and alive. The whole brotherhood must be watchful that the activity of mind and spirit is not drowned by the practical work.

3

To What Do We Want to Educate Our Children?

Education is, first and foremost, the shaping of the child's character. The following quotations help us to understand the main issues involved.

Reverence

ALL MEMBERS of the community have an overwhelming responsibility that can be expressed in the words: *reverence for the Holy Spirit.*

This applies to all parts of the church, but in an especially holy sense it applies to the upbringing of children: reverence for the Holy Spirit, reverence for father and mother – the father, whom God has placed at the head of the family and who, as bearer of the Spirit, must reflect Christ; the mother, who like Mary and the church should also reflect Christ – reverence for the child, for the wonder and mystery of childhood and of becoming like a child;

reverence for the spirit that lives and moves between parents and children; reverence for the church and its services, which is reverence for the Holy Spirit who fills the whole church and all its services.

> The Holy Spirit's gentle breath
> Comes down as wind so free.
> Man's hardened will defies him still –
> He only seeks the child.

Childlike Prayer Life

WE ALWAYS HAVE little children among us, children of three and four or even younger. Many of us find ourselves at the bedside of one of these little children in the evening, feeling his trust and a great and deep love for him. Then we realize how important it is for the child to meet God intimately, and be aware of it. We might begin by telling the child about the stars. We might tell him that on and above these stars there is someone living and good, much more alive than all the animals or people or other children. We will try to help the child to sense that this good and living one can be spoken to and wants to speak to us and help us, that we can talk things over with this good and living one. Then perhaps the child will say, "I know, above the stars are the angels."

"That's right, but above the angels there is someone brighter, better, and more alive. That is so hard to understand that even big grown-up people don't really understand it. It is *God*." Then perhaps the child will have an inkling of what is meant. He will not think about it intellectually, the way adults do, but in his heart he will feel something of the great, good, and living one who is above all things.

Then we can go a step further and say to the child, "And there in your heart, where you in yourself have a feeling for what is good, there is the same great and good one who is above the stars and above the angels. You must feel what this great and living one says, what God says, inside you. Your heart must discover this very great and good one, and then you can speak to him, call on him, be thankful for him, and obey him. The word 'obey' comes from a word that means 'hear' or 'listen to.' If we really hear what the inner voice of the good and living God says in us, if we learn to listen attentively, then we will learn to obey and follow." That is the beginning of real prayer: Thy name be hallowed! Thy will be done! May Thy rule come; the rule that governs the stars and the angels shall rule here too, in my heart, in our lives.

If the child is hungry, he will ask for something to eat; if he has quarreled, he will ask to make it up. And in this way he can be led into the inner meaning of the Lord's Prayer – including the power of evil and quarrelsomeness and hostility, but also the victory over these powers – into the whole of the Lord's Prayer. He may only get an inkling, but perhaps this will have much more meaning than when adults pray their Paternoster two hundred times a day. In many children there certainly is a much livelier sense of what our need is: for God to speak to *us* and for us to be able to call upon God. That is what the childlike spirit really means, and without this childlike spirit no one can find faith and hold on to it, the living faith that, like a little seed, can move mountains.

Gratitude

CHILDREN WHO ARE TOO GOOD are certainly a highly unpleasant phenomenon because their good behavior is unnatural, forced, and hypocritical. But naughty children, those who are unchildlike, presumptuous, disrespectful, and impertinent, are just as unpleasant. The same thing applies to all self-centeredness, even in the pettiest quarrel or clamoring for some supposedly marvelous but actually silly possession.

And another aspect of this unpleasant evil is the chronic indifference and callous ingratitude that some children display toward the good and loving things that are provided for them, often at the cost of great sacrifice. If we pamper our children, they will have a much harder time later on in their relationships with the brotherhood and the church.

Self-Discipline

BOTH AT HOME and in the children's groups, it is important not to get into the habit of being too lenient with the children's moods. Children must learn to take themselves in hand. They must be trained to take a firm stand to what they have done and to express it in a few words. They must not get the feeling they are ill-used if someone has to speak sharply to them. They must learn to face up to what has happened, even if they are shown to be wrong, and not to give half-answers which could mean this or could mean that. They must learn to take a manly attitude and to speak up firmly and clearly.

Freedom to Dare

EVERY GENUINE CHILD wants to dare something and have a fighting attitude. Therefore, where relationships are built on trust between adults and children, as few restrictions as possible will be made on tree-climbing, riding horses, and taking other risks that demand courage.

In this freedom lies the best protection for the child. It is not the over-protection of anxious adults that keeps a child safe but rather leading the child to a sure instinct in dangerous situations and, ultimately, trusting in a watchful care beyond our own power.

Truthfulness and Love

THERE IS NO OTHER TRUTH but love, the love that unites and shows itself in justice and self-sacrifice. If we live by the truth, we will be truthful and courageous in our love. Real love tells the truth. Lies destroy life because they rob us of our integrity and of the relationship of love and trust that unites us. The true life that lives in genuine children rejects lies as it does death. God's life is love and truth.

WHERE THERE is real and true life there is courage. Faith in the truth brings truthfulness. If we live by faith, we live truthfully. If we have no faith in the truth, if we are not loyal to it with whole-hearted devotion, we will be untruthful. Truth makes us upright and determined; it makes us straight in body and soul. That is what it means to have an honest character. That is the upright walk in life that was meant for man. Only the uprightness of pure love creates free souls and leads to truthfulness and justice.

WE WANT TO EDUCATE our children to be orderly, clean, truthful, loving, interested in learning and thinking, and disciplined in body. We can only do this if we, the educators, are so struck by this mystery of God – the child – that we are gripped in our innermost being by the marvel of love and joy slumbering within each child. Whatever activity we take up must cause this holy, living spark to blaze up in us as well as in the child.

Freedom from Possessiveness

IT IS IMPORTANT that children never own anything nor see any of us becoming attached to an accumulation of clothes, books, or other articles. They should see that we are completely detached from the things people usually own and that all rights of disposal mean nothing to us. Children who have grown up in this atmosphere will not be tempted to wound others in any way, whether by bloodshed or murder or deliberate insult. They take a completely clear and firm stand against these spirits of impurity, mammon, and untruth. This attitude can never join forces with hatred and can never ride roughshod over people. Therefore, such a strong spirit of love must be fostered among the children that all lack of feeling, all coldheartedness, all hatefulness and hurting of others are out of the question, even when children have gone beyond the stage of innocence.

NO EDUCATOR has learned all there is to know about this. Every present we give a child as his own tempts him to be unchildlike, to be loveless and unjust. Any time a child lays claim to some possession, it could be the crisis that puts an end to his childhood: the child decides to do something evil that comes from the devil and loses his freedom to forget himself, loses the justice of love forever. When a child reaches the point of succumbing to possessiveness, envy, lust for power, and self-assertion, then he has fallen from the realm of childhood. The thing the child wants to possess, possesses him. In as far as these petty possessions cut him off from these things, he forfeits his open-hearted freedom, his ability to love without stint, and his childlike sense of justice.

Purity

SEXUAL IMPURITY is a most dangerous poison, the worst form of untruthfulness and deceit. It robs us of freedom. Any instance of impurity destroys the very framework of an integrated character. Impurity is untruthfulness and disloyalty; it is sin against the unity between people. Purity, like truth, is the essence of love, the secret of the life that is God himself. The life that comes from God is love in purity and truth.

AT FIRST, while our children are still at the innocent age in which they are not yet fully awakened to good and evil and cannot yet discern between them, we must ask that the whole atmosphere around them may be filled by the Holy Spirit of purity and love. That must be our chief concern; otherwise we shall be guilty of a crime against the children. Secondly, for those children who are slowly awaking to discernment between good and evil, and who of themselves come to decisions and definite ideas, we have to ask that the spirit of God, the spirit that rouses the will, may break in upon them so that their wills become pure, clear, and decided.

The community and the brotherhood must keep faithful watch to see that children from six to sixteen, or even eighteen or nineteen, are completely shielded from anything that would defile their will, which is still innocent, or spoil its budding purity. In no way must any passion be aroused; it would be a crime against this tender age. Once the children are awakened to discriminate between good and evil and their innocence is no longer that of ignorance, they must be protected so that the innocence of a good, pure, unspoiled, and undefiled will is preserved in them. That is education's greatest treasure. May God grant that, when our children have grown to manhood and womanhood, they may enter upon the tasks assigned them in the order of creation with completely pure souls and unblemished bodies.

After the children have chosen to enter this state of innocence, making a decision for good and against evil, it is important for them never to use deceit in any form. An untruthful attitude must be an impossibility in their lives.

ONCE SIN AND GUILT have burst upon the child, causing inner distress, it is essential to strengthen his will and direct his search steadily to the power that alone can free him: that of the purifying and renewing Spirit.

Childlikeness

ONE OF THE STERNEST THINGS Jesus ever said was:
"If anyone corrupts one of these little children, so that
he can no longer be a child, it would be better for him to
be drowned with a millstone around his neck." It would
really be better for him not to live. "Woe to the man
by whom offenses come. If your hand or foot offends
you, chop off that member and throw it away. If your
eye entices you to evil, pluck it out and throw it away."
"Watch that you do not hold little children in contempt,
for I tell you that their angels always have access to my
Father" (Matthew 18:6–10).

Remarkable words! How infinitely deep was the
insight that set these words (about cutting off the hand
or foot and tearing out the eye) next to the words about
children. It is better for a church to have the eye that
oversees everything torn out or the hand that guides cut
off, than for a child to lose his childlike spirit. It would
be better for anyone who corrupts a child and makes him
lose his childlikeness not to live; it really would be better
for us not to live than to corrupt anyone who is childlike
and make him lose his childlike spirit.

That is corruption – to make someone stop being
childlike. Anything that puts an end to childhood is

corruption. Anything that does away with the true nature of the childlike spirit is corruption. That is why Jesus warns us to hold nothing in higher regard than the child, to love nothing more deeply than the childlike spirit, to long for nothing else but to become like children, and never to look down on a child. You look down on a child if you turn him into an emotional, sensual creature who clings to his father or mother or someone else. You despise a child not only when you mislead him to sin but when you in any way deprive him of his childlikeness. You have despised the childlike spirit, the spirit that makes the child a being who sees God. You have looked down on a child, you have had no reverence for his childlike nature the minute you try to make him your emotional property.

IF WE EXPLOIT the child's ability to devote himself to something great by binding him to ourselves and to our own little ego, or to sin, or to selfish gratification, we are corrupting the child and destroying his childlike spirit.

Sympathy for Poverty and Suffering

IT IS NOT TRUE that children have no feeling for the suffering of others, for the injustice and social guilt of our world; the only evidence for such a false view would be children brought up in an artificial environment, removed from reality. But even these children have a longing for the life of a street urchin, for friendship with poor children, which ought to show anyone the error of this opinion.

The awakening child knows about the divided nature of man: the fight *against* himself, against his evil impulses, and the fight *for* himself, for the true calling of man. Thus the child can be awakened at an early age to the mystery of man, for he knows the longing of the human soul and its capacity for devotion. The child lives in expectation, with an inkling of the divine, which is the only way in which the mystery of man can be unveiled. The educator's task of awakening the child to individual men and to all humankind accords with a living concern inherent in the child.

THE CHILDREN'S COMMUNITY should not be exclusive; rather, it needs the strength to receive and include new children in its circle again and again. Children are truly ready to trust and are therefore open at any moment to be friends with a newcomer.

NO WORK WITH CHILDREN is truly alive unless it reaches out toward all humankind. This is so deeply implanted in the children that they have a constant urge to extend their children's community by fighting for and winning others for their group. From their own circle of experience they seek to reach the outside world of children and adults, often very different from their own. These enthusiastic children, the Sun Troop, want to conquer other children's worlds and with them experience fellowship in the common fight.[3]

3 In the early years of the community at Sannerz and the Rhön Bruderhof, "Sun Troop" was the name given by the children to their group of young fighters for Jesus.

4

How Do We Educate?

In an educational community whose guiding power is Christ,
each one, including each child, will find his proper place.
There should be no difference of value in different gifts and
the various kinds of training and work that result from them.

ONE OF THE IMPORTANT obligations of educators
is to place equal value on all the abilities of mind and
body and all the services they render. As early as possible
we must recognize whether a child is chiefly gifted for
physical work or whether his main gifts are in the direction of mental activity, and what kinds of achievement
can be expected of him. From the beginning on, we must
counteract the delusion that some activities have more
value than others that are just as useful in serving the
common good; only then will the child be able to develop
his abilities freely.

A child's particular nature can show itself at a very
early age, even in his play. Every real child devotes himself

entirely to whatever he is doing. The very way a child sees, the astonished wonderment with which he drinks in the things he gazes at, has in it none of the absent-minded indifference and superficiality of most adults. The inner concentration of his gaze shows self-abandonment and self-forgetfulness – the only way to be sensitive to the intrinsic nature of what is seen. The child's play with sand or mud is the earliest stage of experience in shaping matter. Children who are gifted in this way will soon do work of real merit – or, even at an early age, work of artistic value – with paper, modeling clay, wood, or metal.

The transition from play to work is hardly noticeable. In play and craftwork, the young child naturally begins to shape matter and give it artistic form, guided by his creative instinct. For this reason craftwork plays an important role in our educational community. The brothers and sisters who do handicrafts and work projects with the children are just as important to our school as the other teachers, who have the task of awakening the child's mind and spirit in the direction of academic work.

IN THE COMMUNITY, the area of the child's activities as he grows up is the same as that of his future life. He helps in the community farm and workshops; he experiences the contact the church has with the world, and its living, fighting participation in the needs and concerns of the whole world. So from his early years the child lives with all the problems and demands that the suffering of humankind raises.

In a true church life, with the children's community at its core, real freedom is given from the worldwide domination of economics over men's lives today. For here the children live in the community of the Spirit, which permeates all areas of life and work but is neither run by them nor violated by them. And yet in this life community – whose calling is not for its own sake but for the sake of the world, that its need may be overcome – the children get acquainted with the serious problems that arise from the spiritual destitution of the big cities.

Integration of School Subjects

IN OUR CHILDREN'S COMMUNITY we are given a situation that should enable us to build up a school unique in its setup and superior to other educational institutions of our time. In our school, teaching should be on a deeper level, more thorough and more inspiring than anywhere else; it should awaken the children's keen interest and encourage independent and conscientious work. Teachers and children should immerse themselves in the subject matter in such a way that the spirit of faith, love, unity, peace, social justice, and brotherliness sheds light not only on history and literature but, bold as it may sound, on all the other subjects as well. Pascal, among others, has shown us that even very differing subjects can reveal the unity in the universe.

And in our kindergarten and school activities – games, projects, craftwork – our children's community ought to be a shining example of happiness among children, of frankness and trustfulness, of truthfulness and uprightness. At the same time our whole education ought to show a strong spirit of oneness, of community and dedication, a freedom from possessions and self-will, from overbearance, arrogance, conceit, and touchiness, in a way that is not usual among children. Of course, this is possible only when the children are fully governed and led by the spirit of Jesus Christ, the spirit of the church.

WE MUST WORK out the basis for our education very thoroughly and represent the need for all school subjects to be filled by the Spirit. All subjects must come under this unifying Spirit which, coming from the new creation, seeks to permeate the old. In the teaching of world history and the history of literature, and therefore also in the teaching of languages and geography, it is easy to show the ideas of God's oneness, of his undivided justice, the actual powers of his truth and purity – even by their absence – in the course of man's history. But it should also be possible to point to this unifying Spirit of creation and of the new creation in mathematics, physics, chemistry, and in all branches of natural science.

IT IS THEREFORE CLEAR what direction the school has to take in the education of our children. Instead of having to accumulate facts and learn them by heart, the child discovers the inner meaning and connection of these facts. Here the main thing is never the material in itself, neither the subject matter to be learned nor the raw material to be formed into some concrete object. What matters is the creative spirit that masters this material. We do not seek to reach the spirit by way of the material. Rather, we seek to grasp the material through the spirit that animates it, and with this approach the material is really mastered.

Teaching Religion

INSTEAD OF GIVING many examples, we have chosen especially that of religion, because after all, it includes all other examples. We do not base religious instruction on ready-made material. We cannot begin with Bible study, or teaching Christian dogma, let alone the fixed tenets of other religions. With good teaching, the Spirit will be seen behind the history of religion and also behind arts and crafts, social studies, and everything in nature and history. For the Spirit alone gives shape and form to all the workings of God, to the living relationships and the unity that comes from God. So each thing the child studies brings a revelation to him; it gives him a sense of what power, love, and life are. The child comes to understand that this Spirit is alive in each person, in the whole history of humankind, in each national group, in any human community, and in all of nature as well.

Religion is not taught as a specialized subject (dogmas and religious customs); instead, the reality and working of the living God is the starting point from which the children are led to a religious understanding of all areas of life. In this approach to learning, children discover Christ everywhere. He comes close to them as the one who fulfills the longing of humankind's religions through all ages, in all cultures, and on all continents. This brings alive man's history in its religious significance and opens up the Bible to the children.

So the prophets and apostles are seen from the focal point, Christ, in whom everything is possible, in whom

is revealed what is humanly impossible. Then the way
of apostolic discipleship becomes clear – a way bare of
privileges and possessions, a homeless way of love to God
and all humankind, the truly human yet divine way of
life. Here – in Christ and his love, in his kingdom and his
church – is seen the fulfillment of all religious forms and
intuitive religious feelings, the goal of all nature and all
history.

Teaching History

ANYTHING A CHILD EXPERIENCES and sees makes
a vivid impression on him. He is sensitive to the hidden
interrelatedness of all things. The true educator will build
on the child's own experiences to awaken his interest
in historical facts and especially in the history of man's
ideas. Children's own observations of events and facts of
life help them to see the tension that goes into the making
of history: the tension between the grasping will to power
on the one hand, and the generous will to love, which
frees and unites, on the other. A child responds just as
much to the history of ideas, literature, art, and religion
as to apparently more concrete historical facts. Any real
child takes it for granted that the recorded history of
humankind is only an interlude, during which man has

been led away from his original source and yet is being led by God with absolute certainty to his final destiny, which will be completely different from this present interlude.

The Child and Nature

EVERY REAL CHILD lives in and with nature. Wherever he looks, the living soul of nature is immediately obvious to him. It is not hard for the educator to show to the sensitive child the creative power at work everywhere, to point out the relationship of unity in nature, the mutual help, which is the secret of this creation. At the same time, children have to become aware of the dark side of nature, the violent struggle for existence. In every child, there lives right from the beginning a love for the earth, a joy in the starry universe, an enthusiastic interest in the mysteries of atoms and organisms; all this is ready to come to life in each child as love to God and to Christ, the Logos who creates and transforms everything.

AND SO WE REJOICE with the children in their pleasure in nature, their delight in flowers and forest, their happiness in horses, dogs, cows, goats, and rabbits, and their joy in deer and birds and everything else that lives.

CHILDREN do not find God as nature itself, nor in nature. They find him above and behind the whole of nature, behind the entire creation – never in any one part of creation.

ANY EDUCATOR who is truly called to such a task can open up to each child the mystery of birth, the awakening of his childlike spirit and later his adult consciousness, and – last but not least – the mystery of the second birth, which takes place when God breaks into the human heart.

Education and Discipline

WE ADULTS are not capable of recognizing the moment when a child who is still small makes his first really conscious decision to do something wrong.

This admission ought to keep us from the bad practice of wanting to catch a child in a wrong act and punish him then and there. If you distrust a child and read bad motives into his actions, you weaken him instead of strengthening him. To force an awareness of his bad impulses on a child cannot be the living way. Any such attempt harms his inner life; it is brutal; it compels him to be bad. This kind of moral violence – never more out of place than here – causes immorality. No one can take upon himself the right to do that. It is based on the false assumption of a fully developed evil will. It is the educator who has the evil will, not the child. The odds are a hundred to one that when a child does something bad, it is not with anything like the degree of consciousness which the adult assumes, accustomed as he is to evil intentions.

Instead, the true educator strengthens the child's energies for good by starting from the point where the child is completely a child, when he has not yet decided for evil. Our starting point should be where we can clearly see that the child is still full of trust, still able to forget himself completely, still held by the creative power and the love which lie behind all things.

TRUST IN THE MYSTERY of guidance and help from God will lead inner spiritual battles to victory without violence or coercion. All real children follow the leading of their parents, teachers, and others with trust and openness. Strong self-discipline is needed on the part of the educator in order to respond with the same frankness and freedom to the trust shown him. This can only be given again and again in the trust born of faith.

FORCING OR RESTRAINING a child by violent means is replaced by guidance through the Spirit, which awakens and leads each child, on the basis of trust, to test himself freely and courageously in the fight.

Such an inner attitude sees any corporal punishment as a declaration of educational bankruptcy, an admission of our failure to provide the spiritual and truly educational influence for our children. . . . The use of corporal punishment can have no place at all in our education.

With such an inner attitude on the part of the educator it is still possible to exert a forceful influence upon children on various levels of their lives. We can see that a child brought up this way quickly becomes extremely sensitive to any change of mood in his teacher or parent, any increase of determination, or any hasty forming of judgment, even though these emotions may only appear as a change in the tone of voice or a sharpened look. But this should not make us fearful or unsure. To be firm and decisive often is a much greater help to the child in his fight with himself than quietly and all too patiently talking with him about his naughtiness. No two moments are alike. We have to be open and flexible in order to cope with each new situation. Only he is the right man who dares to act when the moment is right. In each child changes are continually taking place: his disposition, his responsiveness and receptivity, his eagerness in the fight, and his capacity for work are all subject to variation.

Education in the Spirit

TO EDUCATE means to awaken. The inner meaning behind all of life should be opened up to the children. Their innate feeling for what is of God within all things and behind all things should be awakened and strengthened.

WE BELIEVE that the awakening of the child's inner life is given through the Holy Spirit. Together with the child, in a trusting way, we take up the inevitable fight against self, which takes place within him at first quite unconsciously, then with growing consciousness. We firmly believe that the childlike spirit will lead to the victory of what is good over what is not so good. We should witness to this autonomy, in which hearts are awakened from within through the spirit of the church in such a way that people can see how here in the church – just as in marriage – autonomy and authority are united.

THE EDUCATION within our children's community is founded on faith in the good spirit at work in all people, and in a special way in all children. On the basis of this faith we stand for the autonomy of the child and of the children's community. By this we do not at all mean that we approve of everything a child may demand or do at the urge of his own impulses. The autonomy we want means awakening the child through the Spirit, leading him to his true calling as a man; it means self-determination of his inner life through the inner light, and the victory of the good spirit over all natural urges, good or bad.

WE HAVE ALWAYS rejected the power of suggestion as a false way. Through suggestion the will of one person is transferred to the will of others, so that a stream of feelings and emotions goes out from one person to others. The power of suggestion is widespread everywhere in churches and schools. We reject it for all our services, including the service of teacher; a teacher represents the whole task of the church in his responsibility for the children: as far as the children are concerned, he has the tasks of a servant of the word and a steward.

How is it then with strength for the service of leadership in the church if suggestion and influence of will are not valid? A solution to this question is to be found only in faith in the Holy Spirit, only in the supreme sanctuary – Jesus Christ. There is no other answer! The Youth Movement does not give it either. The Youth Movement wants the leader to occupy Christ's place in the hearts of the children, to represent what is good. But how is this possible without the guidance of the Holy Spirit? Are we humans capable of this? Even if we knew human nature through and through, would that be enough to enable us to discern what is truly best in the heart of a child and straightaway combat the danger of evil? Are we able to do this with our own powers of good? This kind of education is an ideal beyond human achievement!

Only when we have faith in the Holy Spirit does a true leading through the service of the word take place. Here we have the same concern as we do in our church meetings: that we are united, united in inward listening to the Holy Spirit and in innermost openness for what God is doing.

IT IS JESUS who is the embodiment of love. We do not believe that this love was as natural to any other person, however deeply gripped by the spirit of Christ, as it was to Jesus. It is a miracle when unhappy or inhibited

children become capable men and women – capable in
the deepest sense, in the direction of perfect love, free
from all selfishness. But we do not believe that even the
most gifted educator or the most sensitive psychologist
can bring about such a miracle with the majority of
the unhappy children under his care. *We* cannot save
people from the power of their natural instincts. *We*
cannot redeem them. But the Spirit (which is more than
all our spiritual strength can ever muster) makes use of
us weak people as soon as we stop trusting in our own
strength and in the strength of other people, as soon as
we empty ourselves, open ourselves to him alone, and
hold ourselves constantly open. The final answer does
not lie in education or in the exertion of moral efforts – in
drawing out all the rich resources latent in the tender
inner lives of children and young people. Even the best
and most talented educators and the finest, most sensitive
psychologists cannot, in the face of all the burdens we
inherit, bring about the regeneration and wonderful inner
growth of a truly childlike and pure person.

True, the seed of good lies within each young soul;
true, there is something mysteriously creative in our faith
in this good, through which a trusting and confiding
atmosphere is created; true, the apparently dead seeds

of good can be roused out of their torpidity by the rays
of love and faith; but it has to be very clearly said that
we *cannot in our own strength* develop this courage, this
courageous love, to keep on undertaking new tasks. Even
when we throw all our love into the scales, all our fatherliness and motherliness – that good power given us all by
nature, which was breathed into us by the breath of God
at the first creation and strengthened by the influence
of Christianity and other spiritual values – even then,
with all our love, we cannot prevent human nature from
running wild and going downhill.

To be sure, these good, creative powers are at work
in each person from the time of the first creation, and
we cannot thank God enough for them. Certainly, these
creative powers are the starting point, constantly at work
in an inner way on the spiritual life, bringing people who
are suffering, seeking, and longing closer to each other
inwardly; but the new life and power of the second and
different creation, which *Christ* has brought, bring with
them a quite different love, a greater love, the love of God.
This love springs fresh from his heart into our hearts,
which belong to an aging and degenerating humankind.
This new creation of God, brought by the Holy Spirit, is
more than, and also different from, all the natural love of

our fatherliness and motherliness. This is the gospel, the good news, to every living creature.

The Children's Community and the Sun Troop

THE PRESENCE of the purifying and uniting spirit of Jesus, then, creates community among our children. It awakens in them the desire to build up their children's community or Sun Troop as an expression of the gift of the unity they experience. Just how God's unity comes down to the children, how his power works among them to purify and unite them, will always be a mystery. But in the children's selfless love for everyone, in their generosity and helpfulness, and in their happiness, we feel the blowing of the wind of the Spirit.

In the daily work with our children, the circle of children touched by the Spirit – the Sun Troop – provides the basis of our education. What happens here cannot be taught by any method, let alone improved upon. Here the Spirit is at work so that the children can be true human beings according to God's plan for humankind, for his coming kingdom. Here the children fight for truthfulness, they are true to the cause, they honor God and his creation; above all, they are free.

An adult should never, never abuse the children by forcing his human will on them. The Sun Troop certainly has its own order in the Spirit, which means that its freedom is quite well-defined. They all submit to the Spirit as their only authority, and they challenge each other to follow him. The Sun Troop turns to the Center for its direction in all things. Here, at the Center, the child's innermost life is gripped, and the development of his character, indeed his whole life, is determined by it.

We should not see the children's community as something permanent, like an organization; it is more like a flower that opens to the sun of the Spirit. When the cold mists come and hide the sun, the flower starts to die. When that happens, we are in real need, and the reawakening of life should be the foremost and holy concern of all those who have a task with the children, in fact of the whole brotherhood. At the right moment, the servant of the word will intervene with his inner authority to help this new life awaken.

OUR GREAT JOY is to see a communal spirit come to life in the children again and again, so that the bond between them is one of faith, trust, joy, and brotherly justice. Our little children are a joy when we see in their eyes that they are beginning to trust us and have joy in us.

It is a joy when the older children have the burning faith to use their will to the good to oppose all unfairness or discrimination against others. We rejoice when they join together in little groups or Sun Troops and express their unity and mutual trust in childlike fairness and loyalty. We rejoice in everything new and genuine that springs up then, everything original, not imitated.

RELIGIOUS LIFE in the children's community then becomes free and spontaneous. When the believing church is at work, the children's community awakens. It is a most wonderful thing to live in community with such a group of children. The characteristics of such a children's community are these: a childlike joy in life; a sense of God in nature and reverence for this; a feeling of belonging together; a lively rhythm in their life; not least, an expression of love in work, with astonishing results; and finally, a peculiarly childlike quality in their own religious or inner meetings. Quite naturally, it happens again and again that the children have meetings of their own, a real educational community in the spirit of the believing church.

Anyone would be thoroughly mistaken to think that there are no troubles, no struggles in this children's community. Certainly, it is an outstanding feature of the children's life that they join in joyfully with every part of the communal life that is wholesome for them, for these things reach out to each child from all sides. Yet the children themselves experience their life together as an exercise in overcoming their own nature, in steeling their resistance to all that is evil. And when they learn to recognize and value the *good* in others, it sharpens their vision so that they can combat *evil* in others, and also in themselves.

WHEN THE CHILDREN can live selflessly, forgetful of self, then it is really community and the children are real children. Then it is a true children's community. We must therefore ask God that every encounter of adults with the children serves toward this purpose; this means that each hour must count, whether it is in school during lessons or playtime, or in the kindergarten or baby house, or in doing manual work and crafts. The children's community is the place where it will be evident if we are a church. It is so entirely alive that one could almost say it is the one area that will show if our faith and our life are what they should be; for this is what is most precious, holy, and great. Jesus says: "What you have done to these littlest ones you have done to me"; and, "You will find me in children."

WHEREVER PEOPLE come to full agreement on what they intend to ask God for, *there* is church community. And *children's community* means that the children *agree* in their childlike hearts with regard to anything they may have in mind at a given moment; without much thinking, they simply agree on what they want to do next. Their childlike happiness consists in feeling united about what they want to ask for or do at the moment. That is how they can experience the losing of themselves as individuals in the children's community.

THIS IS WHAT true children are like. It is absolutely crucial for a church of God that its children's community be alive with education that is God-inspired. This will preserve the depth of each child's soul and foster his growth as a being who sees God. Children who grow up in such a children's community see more deeply into God's universe than any adult. The child, in his mysterious closeness to the Spirit, sees God right through the universe without any distraction. He sees God in a way no adult does!

IF A CHILDREN'S COMMUNITY like this is kept living among us, we will understand the reason for those words of Jesus: "You must become like children" – and what a responsibility that is! He also says, "God does not want a *single one* of these children to be lost." God in his love wants the childlike spirit kept unblemished. He wants to embrace the children in this spirit of pure childlikeness within the fold of a children's community.

WE ASK that a real children's community may be protected among us and that it may be given to us over and over again in the family, the baby house, the kindergarten, and the school: a true children's community that belongs to the brotherhood. And we ask that we all may be a part of it, in the childlike spirit of Jesus Christ.

ANY WORK WITH A GROUP of children will bear full fruit only if teachers, parents, and children are part of a community of total sharing – a way of life in which the church of believers draws both children and educators into the true life of the Spirit. The task of this community will always turn anew to children, for we know that in childhood a vivid inner awareness of the mystery of the universe can break through quite directly. This direct inner illumination takes the form of a categorical challenge. The young person has a sense for what is good, together with a certainty that good will triumph. This fires his youthful heart in an ongoing crusade.

As the children of the children's community grow towards adolescence, they adopt a militant stand, which they take up again and again. They feel a revulsion against empty sensuality, which is soulless and irresponsible; they fight against the deadening effect of mechanical jobs; they reject the conscience killing and pleasure seeking of our machine age; they experience the contrast between the church of Jesus Christ and the kingdom of God on the one hand and the unchristian ways of openly imposed violence on the other; they choose liberating rebellion against the lie of a stratified class structure and antisocial business life, and above all against the social injustice of oppressing the dispossessed.

We try to lead our children to a life of unity in the Spirit, to a life of loving service. True unity will dawn within the heart of a child as unconditional love from man to man among those around him; in God's creation, as the goal of God's history, this unity is revealed to him in God's kingdom – the rulership of Jesus Christ. The warp and woof of nature and of humankind, the oneness and mutuality of all life, will become so gloriously clear to our children that, in contrast, the powers of mutual threat and oppression will be revealed as dark and failing and near to death: the blackness is overcome by the resplendence of the light. Everything our children experience in the children's community points to this unshakable expectation of our faith.

Printed in the USA
CPSIA information can be obtained
at www.ICGtesting.com
JSHW080007150824
68134JS00021B/2327